flirtini

a guide to mixing and mingling

allana baroni

clarksonpotter/publishers

new york

Published by Clarkson Potter/Publishers,
New York, New York
Member of the Crown Publishing Group,
a division of Random House, Inc.

CLARKSON N. POTTER is a trademark and
POTTER and colophon are registered trademarks
of Random House, Inc.

Printed in Singapore

Design by Jan Derevjanik

Library of Congress Cataloging-in-Publication Data
Baroni, Allana.
    Flirtini: A Guide to Mixing and Mingling /
Allana Baroni.
1. Cocktails.   2. Cocktail parties.   I. Title.
    TX951 .B265   2003
    641.8'74—dc21   2002155503

ISBN 1-4000-4646-7

10   9   8   7   6   5   4   3

First Edition

This book is dedicated to anyone who sometimes feels like they're on the outside of the "in" crowd. If that's you, find a circle of friends who matter. Then hold on, be real, and party with them 'til you're too old to keep the beat.

party flow

I have Social Disease. I have to go out every night. If I stay home one night I start spreading rumors to my dogs. —ANDY WARHOL

living a stellar social life

Flirtini is a formula for inventing a stellar social life. It's a party permit for spirited hosts and guests, a list of excuses to let loose and the details on how to do it. It's about mixing up a top-shelf scene packed with flirts, skirts, and high-balling. You don't need a PhD to cure common party plagues—you just need a trick or two in your little black bag, the kind we wish were taught in Social Studies 101. Like restoring circulation to the shy guy who's glued to the wallpaper by asking him to be a doll and pass around the Jell-O shooters.

To gather ideas and recipes that morph ordinary hosts into social superheroes, I took off on an international pub crawl. While researching (!) drinks in Paris, Venice, Singapore, St. Moritz, London, and Los Angeles, I soon realized it's not exotic drink recipes that matter, it's the love of a good time, humor, and flirtation that brings people together. Don't get me wrong—a cocktail party needs cocktails. But whether you're celebrating a happy occasion or blowing off some steam, it's all about the opportunity to laugh it up with friends, new and old. Even the most fabulous drink can't accomplish that *alone*.

Ultimately, the most interesting concoction at any gig is a cross-pollinated guest list, and the number one rule of the game is to treat every single one of your guests like a VIP. A party really can change your life in one night. It's the easiest way to meet someone outside your daily loop—someone who could become a lifelong buddy, a business partner, a date, or even a future spouse.

All good parties have a little somethin' special goin' on and usually start with a simple observation. Notice a friend who's down in the dumps? Throw 'em a surprise unbirthday party. Looking for an excuse to invite all the cute golf dudes over? A beer and scotch tasting ought to do the trick. Or, if you recently noticed that you've lost your groove, set up an adult playground of the Caribbean variety to help you get it back! The beauty of these cocktail parties is that they solve life's simple dilemmas while energizing guests to mingle and shamelessly flirt. That's exactly what we're looking for.

If I've learned anything in my years of throwing Hollywood, bling-bling scene parties and blow-outs for my friends it's this: pricey ingredients and weeks of planning do not guarantee fun. Instead, an optimistic attitude and a sense of humor are a host's best assets—everything else is bonus points. Even the most hardened professionals can't control the life of a party, and isn't that the thrill of it?

Behind the curtain of any seamlessly orchestrated party can be a scene of sitcom-style mayhem. Hosting one is like directing live television: anything can happen—and that's the priceless endorphin rush. So don't worry about the screw ups; they can be welcome comic relief. To transform disaster into triumph just think on your toes when the unexpected strikes. Forget the ice cubes? Make it a beer and shooter party. Electricity outage? Break out the fondue, red wine, candles, and your Fifi the French maid accent.

Famous for putting together menus and liquor lists for celebs, movie studio execs, society types, and everyday joes, Alec Lester and Joachim Splichal of Los Angeles–based Patina Restaurant (named *Bon Appétit*/Food Network Restaurateur of the Year for 2002) and Steve Wallace and Mike Escobar of Wally's Liquor in Los Angeles (named the number one fine wines and spirits provider in Los Angeles) were cool enough to brainstorm food and beverage selections for this book. After working with them on many Hollywood movie premieres and social events, I'm stoked that they're a part of these party plans. When you're picking which drinks and nibbles to feature at your party, just know they have been road-tested by the likes of Julia Roberts, George Clooney, Drew Barrymore, and Brad Pitt.

Think of the ten parties in this book as blueprints for rounding out a successful party-throwing career. You don't have to use every idea or follow every suggestion to the letter. They're just springboards to kick your imagination into gear. Serving an apple-flavored Original Sin cocktail without guilt, or a rosemary vodka Transfusion with a great bedside manner has more to do with being a people magnet than a master bartender. It's about cutting loose, expanding your social horizons, and bringing people together.

I hope these party ideas fire you up enough to throw one (or more) of your own. Have a blast!

the party line

There's no magic formula for throwing a killer cocktail party, but here are a few ingredients common to parties where people stay late:

send a shout-out.

The vibe of a party starts with the invitation list. The most memorable bashes forge a cross-section of guests who otherwise might never have the opportunity to mingle. So when you're putting together names for this flirt fest, think of New York City's Central Park—a lush locale where all sorts of people hang out: suits and fashionistas, artists and accountants, punks and plumbers. Of course, you can invite your buds via fax, phone, e-mail, or pager rather than a paper invite—the invitation ideas in this book are purely inspirational. If you have the time and inclination to send an invitation by snail mail, then go for it. The most important thing is to get 'em to the party.

create excuses for mingling.

The whole idea of throwing a party is to mix old pals and new blood. It's absolutely useless if cliques coagulate and huddle. Keep everyone moving and connecting with quick games, interactive activities, and themed parties. The ten parties in this book feature tons of ways to keep the circulation going.

flirt, flirt, flirt.

It's innocent, fun, and exciting. There are ways a host can encourage flirting and things guests can do to make their own magic happen. The techniques are usually basic—from staring contests, slightly naughty toasts, sexy hello's, and a slight touch on the arm to handwriting analysis, fortune-telling, and an immature game of Pass the Orange. The whole idea is to think of flirting as an adventure—you never know what it'll lead to!

make a drink menu.

Ever watch someone squirm when it's his or her turn to order? It's almost like stage fright. Make it easy by announcing everything that's being served. Come up with a list of cocktails and write it on a chalkboard, print it from your computer, or use a grease board and pencil. Knowing what liquor to have on hand also makes it easy on you.

life is too short to stress over crystal and barware.

Unless the queen of England is coming, it really doesn't matter what glasses you use. When everyone is having a blast, nobody cares what they're drinking from. Flip through this book and tag the drinks you want to include in your party. Then see what bar equipment you need for those specific cocktails. Most likely it's just shot glasses, bottle openers, and a cocktail shaker with strainer. Everything else is probably already in your kitchen.

do a sound check.

Music is one of the most important guests at your party. When it works, music is a subtle mood enhancer; when it doesn't, it's a buzz kill. Make sure your sound system is in shape by listening to it from different areas of the party space. Remember that the dull roar of the crowd will drown out some of the music, but make sure the music doesn't drown out the crowd. Preselect tunes so you're not shuffling through your whole collection. Test-drive the playlist while you're setting up.

make a floor plan.

Consider how guests will navigate the party. Make pathways by pushing furniture to the walls, then keep partyers commuting back and forth by placing the bar at one end and the food at the other end of the party. Don't worry about where to set up the bar—a desk, coffee, or dining table can easily morph into a cocktail station.

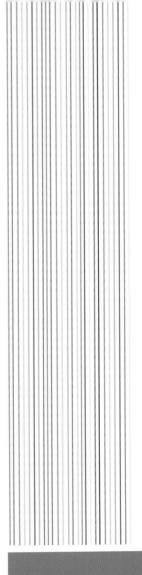

decorate like you learned it at a berlitz course.

Your party shouldn't look as if an art director pulled a week of all-nighters designing it. My parties always look a little messy—I call it that partied-in look. So when
trying to prop out a room, think like a magazine stylist—they go for a mood, not a
makeover. Use the atmosphere ideas in this book as inspiration for utilizing items
you already have, along with items that are easy to obtain. Pick a few areas to
enhance with the theme instead of decking the entire place out.

set the mood with lighting.

Candles are the little black dress of entertaining, so use them wherever you can;
clustered pillars on trays, glass votives lining windowsills, and flickering floaters in
bowls. Swap high-voltage light bulbs with 25- or 40-watt pink versions.

make a smoking section.

If you don't want guests smoking throughout the whole party, then set up a separate area for smoking. Inside or out, make it comfortable, supply plenty of ashtrays,
burn a scented candle, and set out a bowl of mints.

don't make yourself crazy with booze and food.

Include a house specialty drink, then choose a few other favorites to complete the bar.
Most guests will want to try the exotic party drink. Make recipes by the pitcherful and
let guests help themselves so you're not tending bar all
night. It's easier to measure in ounces when making drinks
in bulk, so here are the conversions to the left.

½ ounce = 1 tablespoon

1 ounce = 2 tablespoons

2 ounces = ¼ cup

4 ounces = ½ cup

8 ounces = 1 cup

Count on 1½ pounds of ice per person for a three-hour
party. Remember cubes for drinks as well as bulk ice for

buckets of beers and sodas. Feature a cool nonalcoholic concoction for guests who are pacing themselves and for designated drivers, and serve it in the same glasses everyone else is using.

Cook up the food recipes that you're excited about making from scratch and order the rest from a take-out joint. Then spice up a few grocery store standards with the ideas at the end of each chapter. Don't forget to lay out a few bowls of mints to help flirters get a little closer.

pulling an all-nighter.

If you want to keep the party pumping into the next day, kick it off late (after 11:00 P.M.—club style) and serve breakfast and (preemptive) hangover cures just before first light.

be prepared for guests who have too good a time.

Keep a local taxi company number on speed dial just in case Mr. or Ms. Lightweight has one (or more) too many. In some areas, car clubs offer to pick up guests and tow their cars home so that overenthusiastic partyers don't have to drive to avoid a parking ticket or unscheduled tow the next day. Check this stuff out beforehand so you are Johnny-on-the-spot if needed.

it's not supposed to be work, it's fun—remember?

Ever heard the adage "A project consumes the amount of time allotted to it"? If you give yourself a week to plan a party, then it'll take a week. So plan the party you have time for. If you only have a few hours to set aside for planning, then give the bash you're most prepared for. Proud of your terrace garden? Throw a Garden of Eden bash. Have exotic taste in furniture? Go for a Moroccan Hookah Lounge. You don't have to sweat over every detail and be superprepared. Winging it is part of the fun!

one
blowyourcoat

I can resist everything but temptation.

—OSCAR WILDE

the forbidden fruit party

Temptation—why resist it? By the time spring rolls around, I'm so ready to be released from the bonds of dreary winter that it's pointless to resist an invitation to pull out my strappy, sexy wardrobe and flirt my head off. Spring fever makes shedding layers and feeling attractive pop to the top of the priority list. And because we're likely to be feeling a little frisky, it's the perfect excuse to throw a Garden of Eden party.

booze,
love at first sight

4 lemons

1 750-ml bottle Alizé Red Passion liqueur, chilled

1 750-ml bottle Cognac, chilled

½ cup Cointreau liqueur (or Grand Marnier), chilled

1 cup lemon juice, chilled

2 750-ml bottles of Champagne, or other sparkling white wine, chilled

Slice the lemons into wheels and lay them flat in a container, placing wax paper in between the layers so they don't stick to each other. Freeze the lemon wheels. Pour the Alizé, Cognac, Cointreau, and lemon juice into a large punch bowl and stir. Top with the Champagne, gently stir, then add the frozen lemon wheels to keep the punch chilled.

invite.

Put together an invite that gives your guests a hint of what's to come. Whip up some irresistible copy and put it on a note (handwritten is great). Tie it to the stem of an apple (real or faux) and plop it in a box cushioned with tissue. Here's some sample text:

Be Tempted

Shed your winter coat and come play in Eden.

Drinking, flirting, and dirty dancing

[Insert date, time, location, and RSVP contact information]

atmosphere.

To stir up thoughts of Eden, introduce these enticing scents (they all contain antidepressant properties) by burning candles or incense:

Orange = refreshing   Jasmine = soothing

Patchouli = relaxing   Bergamot = uplifting

Ylang-ylang = stimulating

Since the Garden of Eden was the stage for original sin, when re-creating it, be warned: this party may unleash some repressed inhibitions.

This party can be thrown inside or outside, so first decide where you want everyone to hang. Then look through your loot of garden stuff and see what you can parlay into paradise. I always think about how I'm going to stimulate the six senses—sight, sound, smell, taste, touch, and *humor*.

To create Eden, you don't have to buy out the local nursery; just feature a few key elements. Arrange potted trees, flowers, plants, and ferns into clusters. If you have access to small garden statuary, benches, or birdbaths, intersperse them with the greenery. Raise the kitsch factor by featuring rubber serpents peeking out from the trees, cover table tops with fig leaves (other leaves work, too), and stack apples in urns available at craft stores. You can even throw down some sod (it will last for a couple days and runs about twenty-five cents a square foot—you'll find it at home improvement centers and nurseries, and it can be ordered from your florist).

For more nose candy, float aromatic flowers, such as gardenias or tuberose, in clear glass bowls and place them in spots like the bathroom and the smoking corner. But don't overdose on a ton of different aromas—stick with a single theme, so there is one pleasant smell through the entire party space.

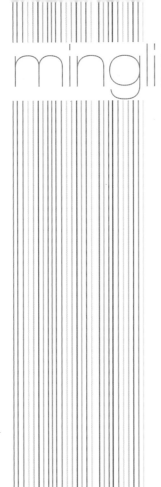

mingling

Transform the tree of knowledge into a tree of free association. Start with an apple tree (or any other tree you can get your hands on—okay, even a coat rack). Attach the forbidden fruit (apples, real or fake) with fishing wire, then tie small envelopes to the tree with ribbon. In the envelopes are calls to flirtatious action. The plan is for partyers to snag an envelope off the tree, cruise over to another guest, and present the envelope. The lucky recipient must then perform whatever task is dictated on the card. Write the keyword (*Truth*, *Dare*, etc.) on the outside of the envelope and put the action on the inside. Here are a few ideas for composing the cards.

Truth: What do you consider sexy?

Dare: I dare you to sing "It's Getting Hot in Here" like Nelly.

Whisper: Whisper your favorite line of romantic poetry.

Confess: If you lived in the Garden of Eden, would you have eaten the forbidden fruit?

Kiss: Kiss your sweetie like it's the first time.

Laugh: Tell a joke with a little innuendo.

Toast: Make a toast to why we shouldn't resist temptation.

Set up a photo op area where guests can pose with the serpent in front of the flirting tree while taking a bite out of a big, red apple. Then snap Polaroids of your guests, stick them into a scrapbook, and ask them to finish the sentence "Paradise is _____."

In general, people feel more secure with something to hold. At a party, it's probably going to be a cocktail glass. Try to make this a conversation starter. One of my funniest ideas came about by accident. Whenever I went to parties where the host was using plastic cups that all looked the same, I would eventually lose track of which one was mine, so I wrote my name on it. Then I started personalizing everyone else's cups, with funny nicknames. My usual alias is "Juanita, Allana's spicy alter ego." If you're using stemmed glassware, print nicknames on small pieces of paper, punch a hole in each in one corner, and string with ribbon. Then let guests pick a nickname that fits them and tie it to the stem of their glass. Have blanks around for guests who want to make up their own moniker.

19

soundtrack.

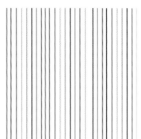

The stakes in that apple caper were high: innocence versus worldliness. Well, where does innocence get you? Exactly. So, raid your local record store for a selection of the sexiest music the club world has to offer. Check the Buddha Bar and Hotel Costes compilations for a sound evoking the Paris late-night scene sipping cocktails from destinations of decadence from Bali to Ibiza. Think Brazil, the sexiest country in the world, with Bebel Gilberto and all the other girls from Ipanema. Think Dimitri from Paris, Nicola Conte from Italy, Koop from Sweden. Thievery Corporation, Zero 7, Suba, Ursula 1000, St. Germain . . . the names are as luscious as the sound.

flirting.

Your eyes are one (or two) of your most important flirting tools. **Eye contact** for more than a second signals interest. So when you spot that supercute stranger while scanning the room, pause your glance until he or she looks your way. If the object of your desire also hits pause, casually make your way over to say hello. **Vocal signals**—tone, pitch, volume, and speed at which words slip out of your mouth—can signal attraction and are more important than what you actually say. Communicate interest with low-pitched, slow, drawn-out words. Compliments are always great icebreakers, sometimes even ice melters. **Touch** is a subtle but powerful form of communication that can be used to convey a variety of messages. In the art of flirting, the safest touch to start with is a light brush on the arm. If you receive a positive response (like moving closer or more eye contact), then later in the conversation, you can edge into the next level, the hand touch.

spring fling rolls

serves 24

24 rice paper wrappers

2 cups cooked cellophane noodles
(follow package directions)

2 cups enoki mushrooms

2 cups bean sprouts

3 carrots, thinly sliced to look like matchsticks

1 cucumber, thinly sliced to look like matchsticks

4 green onions, halved, then thinly sliced to look like matchsticks

Dipping Sauce (see below)

To assemble the rolls, soak a sheet of rice paper in a bowl of warm water until soft. Remove from water and fill with a small amount of each of the above ingredients. Fold one point of the sheet over the filling and roll up, leaving one side open so the ingredients are visible. Cover with a damp cloth while repeating the process with the other rolls.

dipping sauce

Mix ¼ cup soy sauce with ¼ cup rice vinegar and 2 tablespoons sesame oil. Top with 1 tablespoon green onion slivers and 1 teaspoon sesame seeds. Add a dash of dried red pepper flakes or chili oil to spice it up.

grocery store eats.

Fruit doubles as décor and stuff to munch on. So lay out a sexy spread of fresh figs, heaps of grapes, apples, and cherries. Fill in the blanks with aphrodisiac nibbles; grilled asparagus wrapped with prosciutto, steamed artichoke leaves dressed with herbed mayonnaise, and Belgian endive spears topped with Roquefort blue cheese and walnuts. Chocolate-covered cherries or strawberries are perfect to satisfy a sweet tooth.

two
sandboxtime

His groove! The rhythm in which he lives his life!
His pattern of behavior! I threw it off!
—*THE EMPEROR'S NEW GROOVE*

gettin' your groove back.

Has the word *sexy* evaporated from your vocabulary? Has the fun level dropped below zero? Are you wearing triple-digit SPf Stress? If any of this sounds familiar, then you've lost your groove and you need to get it back, baby!

It goes by many names: joie de vivre, mojo, livin' large, getting into the groove. We can't exactly define it, but we sure know when we ain't got it. Although it sounds terminal, it's really temporary. If an actual island vacation isn't in line with your immediate reality, act locally. Book yourself on an escape to a lush, steamy Caribbean atmosphere. In other words, go find your groove in your own sandbox.

booze,
barracuda

serves 20 to 40 (depending on the size of the jar)

Plenty of fresh tropical fruits—watermelon, mango, papaya, etc.

1 large clear glass jug with spicket (usually sold for lemonade)

Vodka—enough to fill the jar

Slice an assortment of fruits and stack them in the jar. Fill up the jug with vodka, cover, and let infuse for two days in the refrigerator (overnight will work if you're short on time). Serve from spicket into shot glasses.

invites,

Charter the party plane and invite some flirtatious, charismatic people on a getaway to your personal paradise. Attach a postcard that has tropical vibe to a pair of colorful rubber flip-flops. Fill out the postcard with the party details. It could go something like this:

Wish you were here . . . so why aren't you? Help me find my groove—discovered missing after a long bout of excessive seriousness.

Dress: Under.

Ideas: Anything that doesn't cover too much skin; these flip-flops, swimsuits, and flowers in your hair are encouraged; puka shells optional.

The vacation starts at [insert time] on [insert date] at [insert location]. Confirm your reservation with Paradise Airlines (operators are standing by). [Insert RSVP date, telephone and/or e-mail information.]

atmosphere,

To make your space look like it's on permanent hiatus, go for a cocktail of bright colors (hot coral, lime green, cool blue, and banana yellow) and play up a few icons of leisure:

Line bare walls with sunset posters and make room for a hammock (they come with stands in case you aren't near any strategically located palm trees). Lay straw mats and colored pillows on a section of the floor. For additional seating use nylon-banded beach chairs from the five-and-dime, rattan chairs, wooden campstools with colored cushions, and lounge chairs if you have them. Anchor the bar with a grass-thatched or calypso umbrella (they sell them at party supply stores). Tie streams of ribbons to its spokes and let them graze the floor.

Once you have the basics, get creative. Laminate squares of fabric, wallpaper, or even pictures of beaches torn from magazines to use as coasters (office supply stores sell laminating sheets that do not require heating). Fill clear glass bubble bowls with live goldfish (donate them to a school after the party). Get your tropical forest goin' on with palm trees, hibiscus bushes, birds-of-paradise, and any other plants that look tropical.

Make sand candles and bottles by spraying them with adhesive and rolling them in sand. Pile tropical fruits in wooden bowls wherever you need a little extra touch.

mingling.

Put on the cruise director hat. Part of getting your groove back is showing other people witty, animated, and sultry sides of your personality. To help coax those characteristics out, inject a few interactive elements into the party:

this little piggy.

Start with something sexy—like toes. Get everyone's in shape by setting up an area for do-it-yourself pedicures. It's a great way to see who you'll want to play footsie with later.

Your guests can show off their freshly pampered toesies with customized flip-flops. Pick up glue and bedazzling supplies; use glass beads, buttons, baby pearls, crystal tattoos, and small stickers. Have some extra flip-flops in case guests forgot the ones you sent.

photo op.

Leave a Polaroid camera around for guests to monkey around with. Then make an instant vacation scrapbook by stringing a clothesline along a wall of the party. Invite guests to hang the Polaroid shots on the clothesline, along with messages scrawled on napkins for other guests. Intersperse souvenirs with the snapshots—straw hats, bikini tops, sunglasses, colorful condoms, drink coasters with lipstick kisses and phone numbers on them, music lyrics, sexy poetry, coconut bras, anything with a floral print.

beat seekers.

A major part of groovin' is dancing. And with a calypso beat happening, it won't be hard to flirt on the dance floor. First push furniture to the walls and make space for the sultry moves. Then, to help get guests (including those who don't have the beat) comfortable with a sexy groove, start the dancing after everyone has had a chance to mingle, drink, and loosen up. As the host, be the first one on the dance floor to get everyone in the mood. Grab a guest or two to join you and you're on your way to finding your groove.

soundtrack.

Seal the sensation of sand between your toes with some Caribbean music. Start with a selection of calypso music from the '50s—it goes a lot deeper than just Harry Belafonte. Check out artists like Mighty Sparrow, and guys who modified their stage names with titles from British aristocracy—Lords Melody, Kitchener, Executor, and Invader; Duke of Iron, Sir Lancelot. Sticking to the decade but puddle-jumping to Jamaica, do a twist on the reggae records everyone's heard by looking for early Wailers and Maytals—back when Bob Marley had a *flat top*. And check out more recent Soca styles for a beat-crazy, tear-up-the-floor tropical sound of brass and sass.

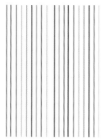

get in the mood. Great flirts exude a sense of fun and have a charming curiosity about other people. Think of it as accessing your childlike characteristics, the ones that break into a happy dance at the sight of other kids to play with in the sandbox. The objective is to consider getting to know people as an adventure, not as something you have to "deal" with.

be yourself. There's a fine line between showing yourself in the best light and being a phony. As Sigmund Freud said, "We leak the truth from every pore," and the world never loves a liar. There's always someone thinner, prettier, richer, smarter, younger, and better connected out there, so give up on that. Instead, exploit whatever it is that makes you YOU: Great joke teller? Use your best material. Smooth dancer? Show us your stuff. Expert scuba diver? Tell your big shark story.

make the first move. I'm not talking about a pickup line. If you see someone you want to meet, don't glue yourself to the wall and hope he or she will magically approach you first. Don't miss out on something great just because you were a big, fat chicken. Put on your confidence cap, walk on over, and introduce yourself. If you get cold feet halfway over, keep moving and just nod hello as you walk on by—then glance back with a smile. If the object of your desire is looking at you, count to ten and then go in for the kill.

skewered shrimp

makes 10 skewers

- 10 branches fresh rosemary
- 1 ripe mango
- 5 dates
- 10 large raw shrimp, peeled and deveined
- ½ tablespoon curry powder
-    Salt and pepper to taste

Cut the rosemary into sprigs 5 inches long. Strip the leaves off 4 inches, leaving 1 inch of leaves on one end. Soak the rosemary skewers for several hours in cold water. Peel the mango and cut into 1-inch cubes. Cut the dates in half, removing the pits. To make it easier to skewer the shrimp, first make a hole in it with a metal or bamboo skewer. Place a date in the curve of each shrimp and thread both onto the rosemary skewer through the hole you've already made. Then thread on mango cube. Season each skewer with a pinch of curry powder, salt, and pepper. To keep the rosemary leaves from burning while grilling, wrap them with foil. Grill the shrimp until pink on the outside and opaque inside, about 5-7 minutes, and then remove foil.

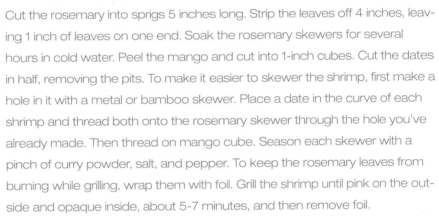

grocery store eats.

Lay out tropical snacks instead of nuts. Think dried mango, papaya, coconut, and banana chips. If you really want to go all out, indulge in island cuisine that complements the skewered shrimp by ordering crab cakes, clams, and other seafood delicacies to be delivered right to your doorstep. Easily available from on-line vendors and through catalogs, just follow the directions on the package to prepare, then lay out newspaper, wood mallets, and tons of hot sauce and invite guests to dig in.

three
afterhours

jazz, booze, and schmooze

Here's the scenario: you're at a dinner or event and for once, everything is going swimmingly—great food, even better wine, captivating conversation. Your date's a perfect 10 and you couldn't be in better spirits. This evening might end happily over morning coffee and the newspaper. It's too early to say uncle and let it end at the doorstep, but not late enough to start making with the quiet innuendos. Do you want to proceed to a loud bar so you can yell nonsensical questions in each other's ears over some thudding club music? No. So throw a mellow after-dinner party at your place with languid jazz and cocktails. I'm not talking bash here. This is about turning your space into a haven from the raucous Saturday Amateur Night and generating a bit of metropolitan sophistication.

booze.

take it black

serves 1

3 ounces vanilla vodka

2 ounces chilled espresso

½ ounce coffee liqueur

Coffee beans for garnish

Club soda (optional)

Fill a cocktail shaker with ice. Add vanilla vodka, espresso, and liqueur, shake, strain into glass, and garnish with coffee beans. To make as a mixed drink, pour all ingredients into an ice-filled glass, top with club soda, and garnish with coffee beans.

cocktail table drinks

Fill a tray with a few bottles of after-dinner staples—Cognac, flavored brandy, scotch, port, and Pernod (a licorice-flavored liqueur). Leave glasses next to the bottles and invite guests to serve themselves.

invites.

Head to a local music store and pick out some sheet music for a great jazz or blues number. In between the lines of music, write in the party details:

After dinner on Saturday night (insert date), swing by my place to mellow out with drinks, dessert, and slow dancing.

[Insert time, location, your name, and RSVP contact information.]

atmosphere.

A small, smoky, intimate club is the vibe. If you don't have dimmer switches, unscrew the 100- and 60-watt bulbs, and replace with the 25- and 15-watt versions (pink and amber-colored bulbs work even more magic). The effect will be a soft glow, the kind that makes everyone look good. Supplement with candles, but not so many that it looks like a gothic shrine. Fill clear glass vases and containers (anything from five to eighteen inches in diameter) halfway with water; drop red food coloring in some, yellow and orange (mixing red and yellow) in others, and float tea candles to create warm and sexy lighting.

Evoke the feel of autumn in New York by adding some lush, deep-colored throws, fabrics, and small lamps with beaded shades. Think purple and green chenille, burgundy and gold satin, and faux fur throws. These touches add lots of richness and require minimal effort (just toss them over furniture). If you want something special on your walls, think about vintage jazz albums—many of them are works of art and look great in frames.

The bar at an after-dinner cocktail party doesn't require much ice, so finding a place for it should be easy. Line the top of a coffee table with sheet music, then make it easy for guests to serve themselves by arranging everything they'll need on top: glasses, liquor, mixers, garnishes, and cocktail napkins.

This party is ripe for cigar and cigarette smoking. Lighting up in public is nearly impossible these days, but at your club, it's actually theme-appropriate. I'm not encouraging the habit, mind you, merely anticipating the likelihood. Instead of banishing smokers to the backyard or fire escape, designate a smoking section

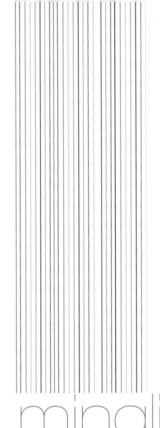

if you think smoke will bother the other guests. Pick a spot that's comfy and has access to ventilation—by the patio door, near a big window, etc. Set out large glass ashtrays (unique originals are available at thrift stores or, in a pinch, any five-and-dime) and an assortment of matches and lighters. Fan out exotic ciga-rettes (the clove kind or the colored-paper variety, found in tobacco stores) in a bowl. Make sure to set out some extra-strong mints, too.

Rifle through an old record collection and come up with an old colorful album that you wouldn't mind sacrificing in the name of style. No vinyl in your music wardrobe? Thrift stores have tons of discarded titles. Preheat the oven to 350 degrees. Clean off the album, oil one side, place the record on a cookie sheet, and bake. After 45 seconds, flip it. After another 45 seconds, take it out and begin mold-ing it into the shape of a bowl (careful that it's not too hot to touch). It's important to work fast on this one, because your window of flexibility is small. After you've shaped it, let it cool completely and fill with chocolate-covered coffee beans, peppermint patties, liquor-filled chocolates, et cetera.

mingling

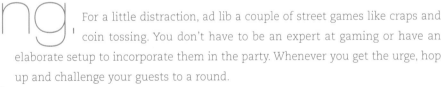

For a little distraction, ad lib a couple of street games like craps and coin tossing. You don't have to be an expert at gaming or have an elaborate setup to incorporate them in the party. Whenever you get the urge, hop up and challenge your guests to a round.

For coin tossing, line people up at a sizable distance from the wall. At "Go," everyone pitches a coin to the wall, and the coin that lands closest to it is the win-ning piece. What the winner gets is up to your guests. I've seen this game played for kisses and even hickeys, so don't be shocked at the wagers!

An old-school street favorite, craps can be played anywhere, so go to it at any available corner of the house. If you're not up for the excitement, you'll have no problem finding takers for a bit of backgammon.

soundtrack,

If you want to go all out, rent a genuine old-fashioned jukebox. They're available through party rental and entertainment companies. Tell them to fill it up with vintage jazz standards and bring it on over!

If you'd rather gather the playlist yourself, stay away from hard bebop; John Coltrane might be a bit much at this hour. This is about the mellow. If you're hitting your marks, then it should be easy to get a few people on their feet for a slow dance. And that's definitely an opportunity to zero in on someone you *like* like. Check out singers Hoagy Carmichael, Ella Fitzgerald, Blossom Dearie, Dinah Washington, Nina Simone, and Ruth Brown. Peruse the Cole Porter compilations. The Impulse and Verve labels are a good place to start. For a twist on those classics, the Verve *Remixed* record is really swinging, and the updated and more DJ-oriented sounds of Koop, St. Germain, or Mo' Horizons are really rich. You can't go wrong with pianists Oscar Peterson, Bud Powell, Thelonius Monk, and Ahmad Jamal. Blakey and Pepper (both Art) had brilliant combos. Add trumpet from Chet Baker and early Miles Davis (the classic *Kind of Blue* and anything from the late '50s period). And try Ben Webster for the deepest sax you can imagine.

flirting,

Setting up a fortune-telling corner can really enhance the vibe. But the twist is that there is no Gypsy lady doing the readings. Guests step in as "Miss Cleo" and make their own predictions: "I see a dark, handsome man in your future. He looks just like me!" Get it together by placing a crystal ball and tarot cards in a little nook, and then encourage guests to take a look into their futures together!

chocolate button cakes

serves 24

2¼ cups dark chocolate chips, divided

½ cup plus 2 tablespoons butter

½ cup plus 2 tablespoons sugar

5 eggs, separated

3 tablespoons flour

5 tablespoons heavy cream

Preheat oven to 300 degrees. Butter an 11 × 14-inch baking pan. In a double boiler, over simmering water, melt 1¾ cups of the chocolate and butter together, stirring constantly, until smooth. Remove from heat and let cool. Mix in the sugar, egg yolks, and flour. In a separate bowl, whisk the egg whites until they form soft peaks, then fold them into the chocolate batter. Pour into the prepared baking dish and bake until firm to the touch, about 20 minutes. Let cool completely. To make the frosting, heat the cream to a strong simmer (just below boiling), then remove from heat and stir in the remaining ½ cup of chocolate until smooth and combined. Let it cool about 30 minutes until thickened. Cut the cake into button sizes by stamping out small rounds with a cookie cutter or the top of a small glass. Spoon frosting over each button and serve at room temperature.

grocery store eats.

Lay out some bite-sized sweets like chocolate-covered coffee beans, candied walnuts, gourmet caramel popcorn, and biscotti. Grab some pre-made chocolate cups and fill them with your favorite ice creams. Add some color with a fresh-fruit bowl and berries for people to munch on.

four
wildstyle

The words of the prophets are written on the subway walls.
—SIMON AND GARFUNKEL, "THE SOUND OF SILENCE"

a hip-hop graffiti scene

We've all seen the handwriting on the wall: the bold signatures of spray-can celebrities. To some, it's visual pollution; to others, a highly evolved form of guerilla art. Even if you think graffiti is a public nuisance, you've probably done it sometime—the instinct to leave some personal imprint that declares, "I was here" (other than a tombstone) is universal. And the illegality of tagging only enhances the appeal. We all want to tell it to the world, but most of us lack either the creative tools or chutzpah to take it wide. At this party, your guests won't say it—they'll *spray* it!

booze.

hipnotic

serves about 12

1 750-ml bottle Hpnotiq liqueur, frozen

1 750-ml bottle citrus vodka, frozen

Lemon wheels for garnish

2 liters club soda, optional

Combine Hpnotiq and vodka in a large pitcher and leave in freezer until just before guests arrive. Serve in short glasses (like a martini) garnished with lemon wheels without ice or in larger, ice-filled glasses topped with club soda.

note ∗ Hpnotiq is a French liqueur popular with the hip-hop crowd. It's made from Cognac, vodka, and tropical fruit juices. It is available where liquor is sold or can be ordered easily if not in stock. It's light blue in color and has a sweet, smooth taste.

invites,

Assemble your crew digitally: Download graffiti images from the net (go to google.com and hit "images," then type "graffitti"); attach your favorite .jpg to your e-mail invitation. Add the party facts (who, what, why, when, where, RSVP) and wait for responses. Don't forget to tell your guests to dress down, because this party gets messy—that's the point.

atmosphere,

You may be looking around your place, wondering how you might turn it into a hangout conducive to creative expression. And you may be wondering whether the stains from your painting fest will ever come out. Think SoHo loft space—get rid of excess furniture, breakables, and stainables. Throw white sheets over your furniture, rest blank canvases on easels (raid toy store for inexpensive ones), and lay dropcloths on the floor to catch any drips (art supply stores carry this kind of stuff).

Got access to a couple of short stepladders? Space two of them about six feet apart and rest planks across the steps to create the bar. New tin paint cans from a hardware store make great ice buckets and containers for bar supplies.

Line a wall of the party area with matte black paper, sold by the roll, for guests to tag up with chalk. Don't use glossy paper because the chalk won't stick. Attach big sheets of plain white paper or muslin (found at art stores) to another wall for the paint and markers. Use blue painter's tape to attach to the wall—it peels off easily (without taking a chunk of wall with it). Use bright paint pens, thick markers, chalk, and acrylic paints with brushes as your tagging tools.

Your job is to help everyone overcome the fear of externalizing those pent-up inner desires. Throw up an outline of lettering and shapes on the canvases and wall coverings for your taggers to fill in. When guests arrive, it looks like the painting has already begun, and they'll get right with it.

If your guests want to tag it and take it, get old jeans, T-shirts, thrift store purses, and athletic shoes and ask your guests to add to the pile. Grab some glittery and puffy fabric paints, paint pens, and markers, available at craft and fabric stores or on-line (keywords *fabric paint* and *graffiti supplies*).

Circulation keeps a party alive. Otherwise gangrene sets in, and

mingling,

you may have to amputate. So keep people on their feet until that appropriately late hour when it's perfectly permissible for people to make out on the couch. There's nothing like some well-placed action magnets to encourage guests to ricochet around the room like atoms in search of a perma-bond. When people are done messing up the walls, make sure there's room for a dance floor.

It's best to have a pro DJ on hand or enlist the help of a friend who's in the know to show guests how to spin and scratch. Use a DJ sign-up sheet and assign twenty-minute sets. Deputize a shy guy to wrangle the next jockey on deck so there's no dead air, giving Mr. Schmoozaphobic a reason to chat people up, and you more time to mix it up with the crowd. If the DJ gear isn't working with your bottom line, then think digitally. People love to exchange the music they're into, so ask guests to bring their picks to spin in your CD player. Two players work best, one for the current tune and the other to cue up—just like a club jockey. Ask to borrow a friend's if you're shy a second. Or put all your party tunes on your MP3 player (in NYC, some clubs are hosting guest iPod DJ'ing).

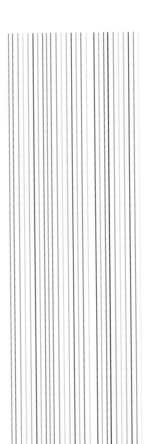

flirting,

Command the intros. One of the easiest ways to get face time with new faces is to bounce around making introductions. Say you spot a pal arriving—hustle her around the room, saying hello to everyone, including someone you have your eye on.

Give people an irresistible excuse to approach you by wearing something unique. Go for an unusual T-shirt, like SCREW YOGA, LET'S DANCE or KILL THE LIVER, IT'S EVIL, or flash your temporary tattoo, which you've applied somewhere inviting.

soundtrack.

This is the perfect opportunity to give props to the old-school hip-hop, and we don't mean last year's Eminem record. We're talking about Grandmaster Flash, the SugarHill Gang, Kurtis Blow, the Fat Boys, Run DMC, Grandmaster Melle Mel, Afrika Bambaata—all those guys who were rapping and scratching when some of us were giggling as our mothers changed our diapers. Did we say guys? Don't forget Salt-N-Pepa and Queen Latifah. Hit fast forward a second and maybe a little Eric B and Rakim, LL Cool J, Boogie Down Productions, or even the Beastie Boys. Go hard with some Public Enemy or NWA or Geto Boys. Go retro-freaky with early Pharcyde, De La Soul, Tribe Called Qwest, Del the Funky Homosapien, and the Roots.

eats.

baby phat potatoes

serves about 20

1¼ pounds baby new potatoes

Salt

Pepper

Toppings can include: green pesto, sour cream, caviar, your favorite cheese, chives, avocado chunks, bacon, mango chutney, or flavored butters

Cook the potatoes in salted boiling water until tender and drain. Or, bake them in a 400-degree oven for 20 minutes or until tender. Let cool and cut a cross on the top. Pinch to open cross and make room for toppings.

Place about ½ cup each of your favorite toppings in bowls next to the potatoes and indulge!

grocery stores eats.

Grab some take-out fried chicken and arrange it on a platter. Then put together a cold sandwich buffet. Grab different breads (baguette, rosemary, dill, walnut, crusty white, etc.) and your favorite toppings: meats like prosciutto, salami, turkey, and mortadella, spreads like pesto, sun-dried tomato paste, and olive puree (tapenade), cheeses like mozzarella, goat, provolone, and Stilton, and extras like roasted peppers, artichoke hearts, and sour pickles. Set everything out on platters or in bowls and baskets, and invite guests to make their own masterpiece sandwich.

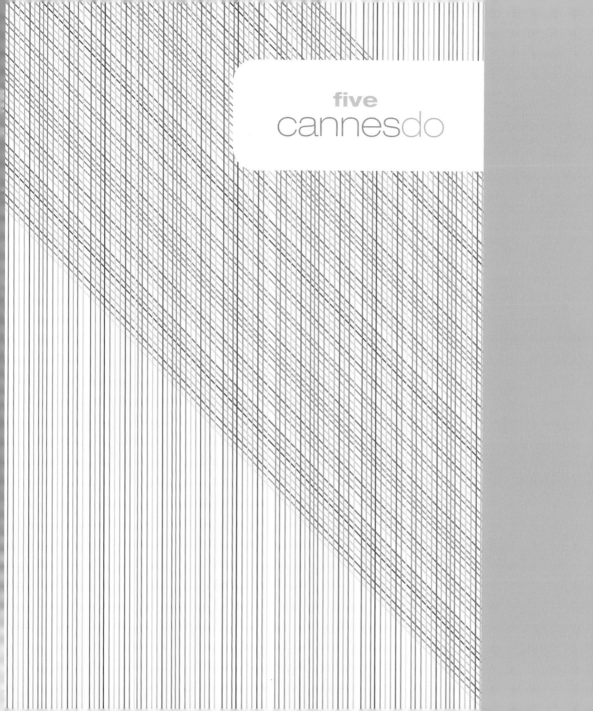

five
cannesdo

I love acting. It is so much more real than life.
—OSCAR WILDE

a film festival costume party

With a worldwide rep as the ultimate in glitz and glamour, the international film festival circuit is part fashion, part schmoozefest, but at heart it's just a partying, people-watching lalapalooza. Get caught up in the fever and host your very own Film Festival Costume Party, and you'll be the star of your own high-concept production. Decide what genre you're going for; if it's a Cannes-style bash, screen some artsy European films. Is Sundance more your style? Then feature indie classics. Or go for a Robert De Niro NYC vibe for a Tribeca festival. Maybe you want to show all the '80s Brat Pack movies, do a Hitchcock night, Hong Kong action night, or a classic horror film festival for Halloween. The possibilities are limited only by the selection at your local video store.

booze.

red carpet

serves 1

- 1¼ ounces tequila
- ½ ounce Triple Sec
- ¼ ounce Chambord liqueur
- 3 ounces margarita mix

Combine all ingredients in a blender with a cup of ice. Pour into glass and serve with a coaster made from red carpet cut into small circles or squares. For extra credit, monogram the drink with a Chambord-infused honey concoction. You'll need a bottle of honey, some Chambord liqueur, and one of those plastic condiment bottles with the fine-tip nozzle found at kitchen supply and grocery stores. Pour the honey into a bowl and stir in enough Chambord to get a deep, red-colored, thick mixture. Fill the bottle with the honey mixture, add the fine-tip cap, and write the drinker's initial on the top of the drink. It works best if you use a wide-mouth glass like a margarita glass so the initial can be seen.

invites,

Grab a bunch of toy slates from a toy store or costume shop (a slate is that thing someone snaps shut like giant false teeth in front of the camera at the beginning of a take—"Scene 2, take 45!") and write the party details on it for your invitation. Or sticker the details to a bag of microwave popcorn (um, unpopped) and throw it in the mail.

Production:	[insert Cannes, Sundance, Tribeca, or your own selected genre] Film Festival and Costume Party
Director:	[insert your name]
Camera:	Come wardrobed as an actor or a member of the press.
Date:	Bring one, on [insert party date]
Scene:	Total, it starts at [insert time]
Take:	Yourself to [insert location]

atmosphere,

Have no fear; getting your pad ready doesn't have to be on a Côte d'Azur scale. Start by rolling out a red carpet by your front door (use red felt instead of real carpet, and secure it by laying a carpet rubber underneath it and a strip of red tape on the edges). Then place his and hers mannequins or dress forms at the entrance, dressed in formal attire for the Cannes event, ski chalet chic for a Sundance feel, or loud, matching track suits for the Tribeca festival. Grab the wardrobe at thrift stores, costume shops, or your best friend's closet. Pick up the mannequins or dress forms at sewing shops, thrift stores, costume shops, or on-line (use keywords *mannequins* or *dress forms*).

Transport your sofa back to the feeling of the old movie theaters by draping red velvet fabric over it. And if you need extra seating but don't feel like your IKEA chairs measure up, just throw some lush red velvet over 'em.

Deck the walls with movie posters, and around the party space, casually arrange tabloids mixed in with glossy rags that celebrate the celebrity lifestyle. I'm talking *InStyle, People, Vanity Fair, Us,* and *Variety.*

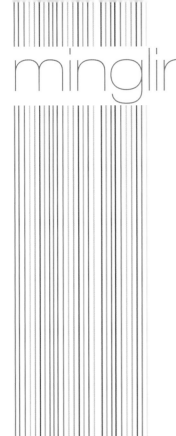

mingling.

Party cam! Remember the mannequin greeters from the party entrance? Stand an easel next to them that holds cue cards featuring questions like "Who's your agent?" and "Who are you wearing?" Set up a digital camera and capture your friends' grand entrances, or have disposable cameras on hand to get flashbulbs popping.

the seventh-inning stretch.

A movie's running time might turn your schmoozefest into a snoozefest. Break the night up with a few things to keep guests interacting. Let people stretch their legs (and their concentration) a bit with some popcorn bucket decorating with magazine photos, movie ads, and paparazzi shots. Grab markers, glitter, glue, and stickers, spread them all out on the coffee table, and let your guests go to town. Everyone can personalize a bucket and take it home for their own movie nights.

drinking games:

Genre films tend to have repetitive features, which scream out for a drinking game. On Cannes night, everyone drinks when a subtitle misses the mark (my favorite's from an old Jet Li movie—"It's a holy war against the bad eggs!"). Obviously, on Tribeca night, the cue is when someone gets whacked. Most indie films include multiple moments where a character makes a speech about not fitting in—everyone take a shot!

Try a game called Six Degrees of Separation. Pick a starting point and have that guest announce the name of a movie. The person sitting next to that person must name an actor that appeared in it. The next person must then name another movie that actor appeared in. Going around the room, each person's got to name another actor who appeared in that movie, then a movie the last-named actor appeared in, then another actor who appeared in it. And so on. Those struck with brain freeze get an "M." Five strikes and you're out—in other words, if you can spell M.O.V.I.E., you're outta the game.

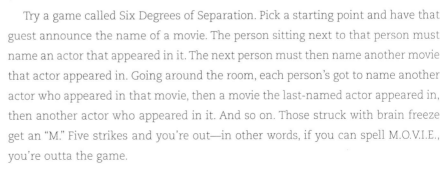

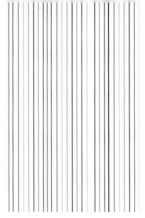

"I'd like to thank the Academy": Make like the pros and honor your guests with a mini awards ceremony. Present an award to the guest who wins one of the games. Give a statuette and invite the winner to make a speech. Pick up the statues at costume shops or trophy or toy stores. Be sure to cut them off after a minute and a half.

Perform a hand/footprint signature ceremony just like they did for the bigwigs at Grauman's Chinese Theatre. Be sure to cut them off after one and a half minutes. Just grab some plaster of Paris at a local art store, mix according to the directions, and shovel the glop into one of those low cardboard boxes they ship sodas in.

soundtrack.

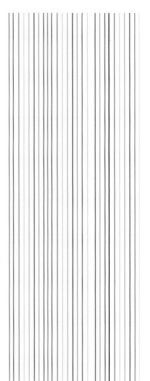

The soundtrack to this party will mostly be the movies themselves. But once you shut off the screen (or turn down the volume), keep the party rolling with selections from the soundtrack section of your local record store.

For a Sundance-themed party, go with the soundtrack from *Swingers*, *Ghost World*, *200 Cigarettes*, *Hedwig and the Angry Inch*, or *SLC Punk!*. For Tribeca, *Big Night* adds a little Italian flavor, *GoodFellas* is filled with great '70s music, and all of Spike Lee's films have great soundtracks. Cannes is an international movie festival, so you don't have to limit yourself to French film music like the *Amélie* soundtrack, *CQ*, or the *Arthouse Café* classic film music series. Anything from *Run, Lola, Run* to *Buena Vista Social Club* to Nino Rota's classic film music for Fellini will do.

For music that fits in with other movie genres, try the *Jackie Brown* and *Pulp Fiction* soundtracks from the House of Tarantino or the high-energy *Trainspotting* soundtrack. Any of the Austin Powers soundtracks are fun; so is *Moulin Rouge*. Go for *Velvet Goldmine* or *Detroit Rock City* for some glam rock nostalgia. A collection of James Bond themes never goes awry. And don't forget party standbys *Purple Rain* and *Saturday Night Fever*. If you're yearning for the taste of hayseed, *O Brother, Where Art Thou?* is perfect.

oscarnight.

This party also makes for an amazing Oscar-night party (have your tube tuned to the ceremony instead of screening movies). If you opt for an Oscar party, a lot of magazines and Web sites print out Oscar scorecards; you can send a copy with your invitation. Get the Oscar theme going by dressing up the floors with a Walk of Fame. Trace stars onto a canvas strip the length of the area you want to dress. Found at fabric and artist's supply stores, canvas is a thick and inexpensive material. Paint the stars red and label them with your friends' names instead of celebs'. Keep the walkway free of slip-ups by laying a rubber mat underneath.

flirting.

Think autograph hounds. Encourage a little saucy handwriting analysis. Guests ask one another for an autograph, and then explain what the handwriting says about them. Pick up a handwriting analysis book that will reveal intimate traits and secret passions. "This loop means you are open to new experiences"—that's an open invitation to flirtation.

tomato crisps

serves 8

- ¼ cup olive oil
- ¼ cup diced fresh mozzarella
- salt and pepper, to taste
- 2 juicy tomatoes (heirloom are great), sliced
- 1 loaf ciabatta bread (white crusty Italian bread)
- 2 tablespoons fresh thyme leaves
- 2 tablespoons sliced basil

Drizzle some olive oil over the mozzarella and sprinkle with salt and freshly ground pepper. Slice the tomatoes, drizzle with olive oil, and sprinkle with salt. Slice the bread into eight ½-inch-thick slices. Drizzle the bread with olive oil, sprinkle with thyme leaves, and bake in a 350-degree oven until golden. Top the toast with the sliced tomato, some mozzarella, and sliced basil.

grocery store eats.

Caviar does not have to be fussy or pricey. Check out what's available at markets or delis in your area. Whitefish, trout, salmon, or lumpfish roe are great substitutes for Beluga. Just put it in a small glass bowl, place it in the middle of a platter, and surround it with gourmet potato chips to scoop it up. Dress up store-bought popcorn by mixing it with melted butter, fresh chopped rosemary, grated Parmesan cheese, and freshly cracked black pepper.

six

backstagepass

Rock and roll is an expression of the energy of life,
the energy that comes from the realization you're alive,
projecting it outwards. You just wanna stamp your feet and
wave your hands in the air. —IAN ASTBURY, THE CULT

a rock-and-roll karaoke lounge

It's *not* only rock and roll—oh, Mick, it's so much more. Music is a powerful,

mood-altering stimulant that blows the mind, body, and emotions as no

other art form can. With beats that run from sensual to pounding, and lyrics

that range from cute double entendres to blatant come-ons, rock music has

fired our imagination and fueled our most primitive activities for more than

fifty years. Plus, it's really noisy. Maybe that's why rock and roll continues to

get people so hot and bothered. So, if you're feeling the need for a little heat,

crank up the amp, get your head in garage band mode, and set up for your

Rock-and-Roll Karaoke Lounge.

booze.

speedball

serves 1

- 1 ounce rum
- 1 ounce Jägermeister
- ½ ounce lime juice

  Cola

  Lime wedge, for garnish

Pour rum, Jägermeister, and lime juice into an ice-filled glass.

Top up with cola and garnish with a lime wedge.

invites,

Make your own all-access passes to send as invitations. Start with two- by three-inch pieces of card stock or poster board. Put the words *All Access* and the party date and details on one side, and an appropriate picture torn from a magazine on the other. You can even personalize these for each guest with funny photos, etc. Then laminate the invites with sheets sold at office supply stores that don't require heat. Punch a hole at the top and attach it to a cord (shoelace, whatever) long enough for someone to throw around his or her neck, so it looks like the coveted laminated pass that gets insiders backstage at big events.

atmosphere,

Customize the backstage area by using rock's iconic symbols as your muse for designing the lounge. Just like an underground club, make those who made your list feel super VIP by posting a security dude out front. He doesn't have to be real; a buffed-out mannequin, stuffed gorilla, or blow-up Godzilla can pull off the intimidation thing.

Transform a guitar case into the bar by lining it with funky fabrics (stake out the fabric stores for Day-Glo fake fur, bright purple velvet, or silver sequins). Pick up the case at stores that sell musical instruments or thrift stores or pawnshops—then glue, staple, or pin the fabric in place. Next, fill it up with the bar essentials: plastic cups, napkins, ice bucket, booze, mixers, lemons and limes.

If budget and space allow, set up a small stage for karaoke performances. Party rental companies have all the supplies and will set it up for you. Start with a platform (4' × 4' × 1') to make the stage. Angle a light to make it look like a spotlight is shining on the stage and add a sequin fabric backdrop to get the total look. Cover the stage floor with a furry rug and a mike stand tied with scarves à la Aerosmith. If a stage setup doesn't fit into your scheme, just lay down the furry rug to mark the spot for the karaoke area.

If you can, get hold of a small drum set or congas for the back of the platform, and have a guitar, tambourine, or some funny kiddie instruments on hand (for

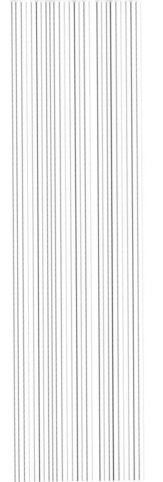

guests who'd rather be in the background). Put a full-length mirror near the stage area for one last "I look hot" glance before picking up the mike. Clear the front for a mosh pit, then toss floor pillows in the corners in case the mood gets mellow. Don't stress if laying out the bones for everything on your wish list isn't in the budgie—find what you can do and go for it. All you really need is space for guests to get their shot at the mike and ham it up—everything else is whipped cream.

To help with that self-conscious star/anonymity thing, swap out the screeching white lights for blue, green, and red party bulbs and cover plain lampshades by wrapping them in loud fabrics. (Use Velcro tape found at fabric stores to attach the fabric. Place the sticky sides of the tape on fabric so you don't damage your shade, then overlap for a snug fit.)

Have you ever noticed how everyone gets pumped up when someone in

mingling,

the crowd steps out of his or her conventional persona and really cuts loose? Or how people become heroes when they have the guts to do something intentionally embarrassing? That's the vicious appeal of karaoke, our favorite Asian import since compact cars. It's instant glee to watch the most unlikely wallflowers suddenly turn into Entertainer of the Year when the mike is handed to them. It's even better when they really suck, know it, and don't care! Unveiling secret aspirations and throwing ego out the door put people at ease—and inspire the otherwise timid to pull back the shower curtain.

Setting up a karaoke machine is super easy. You can rent or purchase one along with tons of music titles (electronics stores sell the machines and music discs; party-throwing companies and some DJs rent everything you'll need). The machine is connected to your TV so the lyrics appear on your set's screen. Pass out cheap lighters for fans to flick during dramatic renditions of anthems, and panties to toss on stage when performers get hot.

Have your camcorder ready to capture those missed notes and flubbed lines. Burn the highlights on a CD, or put them on your Web site (or maybe collect some blackmail money *not* to!).

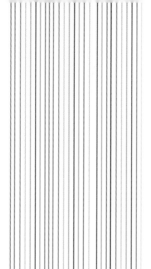

undress the dressing room.

Since the term *rock and roll* really means S-E-X, it's hard not to feel sexy when you get caught up in the energy of a rocking party. And since music and fashion are a beast with two backs, this is the time to cull your ensemble from your sexy, groupie corner of the closet. That doesn't mean showing as much skin as possible; it's more about wearing what makes you *feel* sexy. Whether it's your favorite pair of jeans—the ones that make your butt look like a happy face—or your slinkiest, sheerest black lace, the dress code for this party is confidence.

Have a few tokens of rock stardom around so guests can augment their look—temporary tattoos, salad-plate sunglasses, flamboyant wigs in unnatural colors, beaded chokers, and leather anything will get the talent pool to lose stage fright.

soundtrack.

For some, rock and roll equals Chuck Berry; others apply the moniker to anyone from the Rolling Stones to Green Day. The karaoke will fill most of the party, so your time to rock is short; don't waste it. As we go to press, a retro wave of noise is upwelling (the Strokes, the Hives, and the White Stripes). But most of the rock that rocks is a lot older than that. The point is this: your rock is your rock, whether it's the Velvet Underground, the Stooges, the New York Dolls, or the Ramones; the Who, Pink Floyd, the Kinks, or the Yardbirds; T. Rex or Metallica, Aerosmith or Roxy Music, Bowie or Buzzcocks, Nirvana or Van Halen, Anthrax or AC/DC, Korn or the Clash, Led Zeppelin or ZZ Top, Guns N' Roses or the Police. Just don't let it die.

flirting.

Enthusiasm is incredibly attractive. Check out Bobbie Fleckman in *This Is Spinal Tap* (Fran Drescher's breakout role)—"Hi, I'm Bobbie Fleckman . . . hi, Bobbie Fleckman . . . hi." She was hilariously over the top, but take a page from the careers of successful music executives—work the room, remember everyone's name, and they'll remember you. If the art of chat isn't in your repertoire, try another approach. As the king of rock and roll said, "A little less conversation and a little more action." Dancing is the ultimate opportunity to flirt. So if the kitty's got your tongue, pull out those Elvis moves. Nothing gets the party going faster.

groupie burgers

makes 8 mini burgers

½ pound lean ground beef seasoned with salt and pepper

2 slices cheddar cheese cut in quarters

8 mini hamburger buns (sesame-encrusted ones are best)

¼ cup of chili, heated

4 cherry tomatoes, halved

8 leaves lettuce

8 slices pickles

Form beef into 2-inch patties ½ inch thick. Sauté until cooked to desired degree (medium, well done, etc.), top with a slice of the quartered cheese, and place on the bottom of a bun. Top with a small dollop of chili, a tomato half, a leaf of lettuce, and a slice of pickle, and top with the other half of the bun.

grocery store eats.

Grab big bags of M&M's and separate them into their own color lot. Give the green ones to guests who need a little help in the flirting department!

Spice up 5 cups of canned mixed nuts by warming them in a 350-degree oven for 8 to 10 minutes. Then toss them in a mixture of 2 tablespoons melted butter, ¼ cup chopped fresh rosemary, ½ teaspoon cayenne pepper, 1 tablespoon salt (if they are not salted already), and 1 tablespoon dark brown sugar. Pick up spiced, frozen french fries and bake them according to the package directions. Then form cones out of pages from *Rolling Stone* magazine and stuff them with the crisp fries. Just roll the paper into a cone and secure the edge with tape or a sticker.

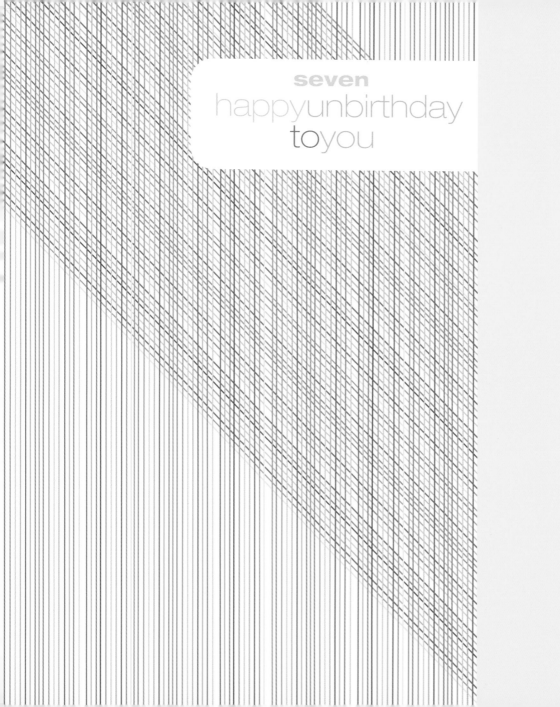

seven

happyunbirthday
toyou

Imagine just one birthday every year. Ah, but there are 364 unbirthdays.
—"THE UNBIRTHDAY SONG," FROM *ALICE'S ADVENTURES IN WONDERLAND*

a surprise mad tea party

How do you rescue a friend in a blue funk and in desperate need of a booster shot to the ego? Whatever the reason, everyone needs to be pumped up a bit now and then. "Honey, it's gonna work itself out" is all very nice, but why not put a party where your mouth is? You'll make 'em feel ten feet tall while they're getting back on their feet. Enter, the event that dissolves even the funkiest of funks and pump-primes the most deflated of egos: the Unbirthday Party. This is like an intervention, but nobody's misbehaved—yet. On our actual birthdays, expectation sometimes sets the stage for a tragedy of errors. Here, there's no pressure. Your unfortunate friend isn't expecting anything (except maybe more bad luck). So the key element of this mission is surprise. Get into stealth mode, round up the troops, and rally them for a karmic intervention.

booze.

citrus caterpillar

serves about 25

- 1 750-ml bottle Limoncello liqueur

- 1 750-ml bottle citrus vodka

- ¼ cup of simple syrup (see Note)

  Lemon peel or wheels for garnish

  Club soda (optional)

Combine Limoncello and vodka in a large pitcher and leave in freezer until just before guests arrive. Pour into teapots and leave in the center of your birthday table. Serve in short glasses or teacups (like a martini) without ice or in larger ice-filled glasses topped with club soda. Garnish both with lemon peel or wheels.

note *To make simple syrup, mix 1 cup sugar and 1 cup water together. Heat until boiling, then simmer until sugar dissolves. Cool.

invites,

Take a close-up photo of a clock or watch with the hands indicating the time that you want guests to arrive, then paper-clip the photo to a card with all the details. Sample text:

"Don't be late, it's a very important date. We're having a surprise unbirthday party for [insert name of unfortunate funked-up friend]. Wear your play clothes, bring a toast, and come over to my mad playhouse. It's on [insert date, time, and location]. Don't worry about wrapping a present; we'll have the stuff to decorate boxes here. For extra credit dress like [insert unbirthday person's name]. RSVP to [insert contact telephone number and/or e-mail address].

Use a plain brown lunch bag as the envelope—leave it flat, slip the card in, and secure the opening with stickers.

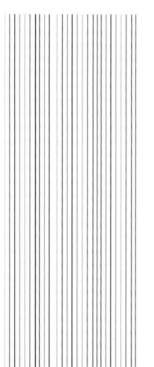

atmosphere,

It's a mad playroom theme, so focus the décor on the party table and re-creating the kind of unapologetic fun you had when you were a kid.

Here's a trick for making a no-sew tablecloth: wrap colorful fabric around the edges of the table, letting the bottom edge of the fabric just touch the floor. Secure the top edge of the fabric by taping it to the tabletop with blue painter's tape (it's not as sticky as duct tape, so it won't hurt delicate surfaces). Lay a length of fabric over the top of the table to hide the blue tape (make sure the width of the fabric is wider than the width of your tabletop). Finish the edges by gluing or stapling fringe, ribbon, or beaded trims. Open inexpensive paper umbrellas or Chinese paper lanterns and hang them from the ceiling over the party table for some added color.

Set your mad tea party with platters of tea sandwiches, fondue fixins, dessert-sized plates, cups and saucers, and as many teapots as you can scramble together. Customize plain highball glasses by studding them with tiny jeweled stickers (the bindi versions work perfectly). Accent the rest of the table with candles, greenery (like miniature roses in terra-cotta pots), an imperial throne at the head of the table for the unbirthday boy or girl, plus pennies, stars, small bells, cat's-eye marbles, goldfish, and frog-shaped charms—all thought to bring good luck.

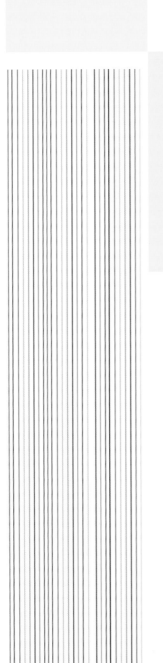

flirting.

Be immature. Okay, so you're immature a lot of the time, but at this party, it's appropriate. As host to a party that encourages fully grown adults to let their inner wild child run free, get your guests on the flirt track with a few childish games. Remember Pass the Orange from fourth grade (or maybe a recent drunken trip to Club Med)? Hold an orange under your chin and pass it to Mr. or Ms. Irresistibly Good Looking, who has to grab it from you without using any hands—Oh, behave!

How about musical chairs? You might think it's only for kids, but when the music stops and you're left sitting on the lap of young Dr. Hottie or Fireman Steve, you'll change your mind.

mingling.

Up the atmosphere of juvenile fun with some interactive elements, like a present-wrapping station. Set out white butcher and brown craft paper. Then leave ribbons, markers, stickers, rubber stamps, ink pads, etc., to decorate the paper. Leave a Polaroid camera close by, guests can take pictures of each other and attach them to their presents as a card. Open a trunk and stuff it with all sorts of crazy hats to overflowing proportions—Mad Hatter top hats, strange vintage toppers, a royal crown or tiara for the guest of honor, and maybe a cape. Lay out a court to shoot a game of marbles, an area for a tournament of jacks, and a table for Chinese checkers. Hang a piñata stuffed with fortune cookies for guests to replay their favorite at-bats from baseball games. To set a full-on fantasy mood, rent the movie *Alice in Wonderland* and let it play on your TV throughout the party.

Toast (kind of like a roast, but nicer) the guest of honor by singing "The Unbirthday Song" from *Alice in Wonderland* as cupcakes and candles are wheeled out (you'll find the song in the mad tea party scene in the movie). Then go around the table for individual toasts.

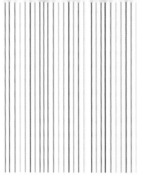

soundtrack

The music's role in this rescue mission is to temporarily suspend the burdens of adulthood and make everyone feel like kids again. All kids' music shares the same ingredients list: kindergarten-simple rhymes, shiny melodies, and upright beats. It must feel like a piece of pink candy popping in your mouth. The Beatles made the best kids' music ever, even during their darkest hallucinogenic period while they tried to locate the get-out clause in their deal with superstardom (I'm talking about the White Album—hello, "Ob-La-Di, Ob-La-Da"). Most of all, it's nearly impossible to sustain a crabby face against an assault of those Lennon-McCartney truffles of popular joy. If you don't have one of the thousands of collections out there, get one now—you might need it yourself sometime.

tower of cupcakes

cupcakes

¾	cup unsalted butter
1½	cups sugar
6	large egg yolks
4½	teaspoons baking powder
3	cups cake flour
1¼	teaspoons vanilla extract
1	cup milk

buttercream frosting

3	cups powdered sugar, sifted
¼	cup milk
¼	cup unsalted butter, softened
1	teaspoon vanilla extract
	Pinch of salt
	Assorted food coloring

Preheat the oven to 350 degrees. Cream the butter and sugar together until well combined. Add yolks one at a time until thoroughly incorporated. Sift the baking powder and flour together and fold into mix along with the vanilla extract. Add milk slowly and stir until fully incorporated. Fill 18 paper-lined muffin tins two-thirds of the way up (make in 2 batches if necessary) and bake for 20 to 25 minutes. For the frosting, blend all of the ingredients using a handheld mixer in a bowl until smooth and fluffy. Separate into batches and add different food colorings for variations in color. Top cooled cupcakes with buttercream frosting. Then add candles for the unbirthday ceremony.

grocery store eats.

If you have fondue pots, grab some prepared cheese fondue, follow directions on the package and serve with cubes of bread, artichoke hearts, pear wedges, etc. Throw together some tea sandwiches, such as cucumber and cream cheese, mini-BLTs, goat cheese and chive, chicken salad—and don't forget to include peanut butter and jelly (excellent without the crust). Go wild with snacks from your childhood: Tater Tots, chicken fingers, mini pot pies, etc.

eight

hookahlounging

smokin', drinkin', and playin'...moroccan style

Even if you've never traveled to Turkey, the Middle East, or the southern Mediterranean, you've probably seen a hookah—the Caterpillar puffed one in *Alice in Wonderland*. It's a decorative water pipe with an elephantine hose, long enough to stretch across a table. Devotees generally mix a small amount of tobacco with fruit- and flower-flavored molasses. With six feet of water filtration, it eliminates the negative sensations one gets from smoking cigars and cigarettes. More a social ritual than an excuse to fill one's lungs with smoke, the hookah makes a nice centerpiece for an intimate evening shared with friends. Add a few exotic touches, and you will transport your guests on a magic carpet far away from an otherwise dull and ordinary Saturday night.

booze,
moroccan mojito

serves 1

    3 sprigs mint

    2 ounces light rum

    2 ounces simple syrup (see p. 67)

       Club soda

    1 cardamom pod

Muddle (smash) the mint leaves, rum, and simple syrup together in the bottom of a mixing glass with the back of a spoon to release the flavor of the mint. Pour into a tall glass filled with ice, top with club soda, and garnish with more mint and a cardamom seed.

note ★ Since mint tea is Morocco's favorite drink, I like to make loads of this spiked version in a teapot, then pour from very high into colorful, gold-trimmed glasses. I usually spill some, but it's just part of the deal.

invites.

Come with me to the Kasbah . . . Send a combo invitation and advance party favor to get your harem of friends in the mood. Look on-line or in costume shops or exotic goods stores for toe rings or babouche slippers (pointed Moroccan slippers worn by both men and women), finger cymbals (used by belly dancers to keep the beat), or a fez (a round red hat with a tassel).

Forward the details with a simple note pinned to the item:

Want to take a ride on my magic carpet? Drop in for a smoke at the Kasbah. It's happening on [insert date, time] at [insert location]. Wear whatever makes you feel like belly dancing. Let me know if you're on board. [Insert RSVP date and contact information.] See you there. [Insert your name], The Sultan of Sin!

atmosphere.

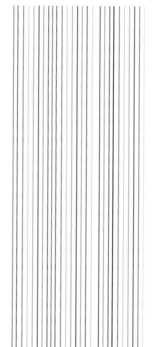

Don't stress about capturing the exotic aura of Morocco. It's about creating a mood, a hint of the culture. Arab, Indian, Spanish, and Mediterranean accents all get the point across. Pick the design ideas that work with your dreamscape, burn some incense, charm some snakes, and go Technicolor with this party.

While taking their sheep to pasture, Berber shepherds live in striped tents. Lined inside with colorful fabric wall coverings, loads of carpets, and piles of large pillows to relax and sleep on, they are used by Moroccan city dwellers for garden parties.

To re-create the Berber tent feeling, use lightweight green and pink synthetic chiffon (available at most fabric stores). It's inexpensive and easy to secure to the ceiling with tiny pins. For a billowing look, start by securing the corners of one end of the fabric with push pins. Let it hang two or three feet down and three to four feet across the ceiling until you cover the area you are dressing up. Pin the same sheer fabric in a different color to the walls (or use flat sheets if that's easier). Just attach it near the ceiling and let it fall where it may. For a similar effect, use those mosquito-netted canopies (meant to be placed over the headboard of a bed) to accent a seating area. They're inexpensive and can be found in bed and bath shops.

To make a Moroccan family table, assemble a low table with floor pillows thrown

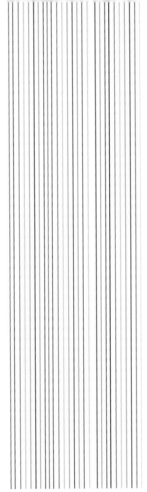

around it by placing a makeshift tabletop (a piece of plywood, a few planks squeezed together, etc.) on top of four piles of books. Drape an opulent, jewel-tone fabric (inexpensive versions aren't hard to find) over the top. Accent the party landscape with bowls of oranges wherever an extra touch is needed.

Grab some wilting, half-price roses and scatter the petals on tables, in bowls of water, on the floor at the entrance to the party.

Now that the room looks the part, you're ready for action. Ensure the # mingling.

hookah is in service all night by getting your supplies organized beforehand. Look for the hookah pipe and tobacco at head shops, on-line, or in Middle Eastern stores and markets. Rentals are often available, as well as inexpensive versions. And it's perfectly okay to ask salespeople how to use it. You'll need an assortment of fruit-flavored tobaccos (some popular flavors are apple, jasmine, rose, mint, mango, and strawberry), charcoals to keep the tobacco smoldering (these are small discs that fit hookahs and incense burners), some additional mouthpieces, and a lighter.

Incite guests to decorate bare belly buttons, sexy ankles, and bulging biceps with henna body art; kits are widely available these days at costume shops, beauty supply houses, and on-line (use keyword *henna*). Then set up an area with the stencils and henna.

Start the belly dancing after some booze has gone down—guests will be a little bolder. Ask around at a local Middle Eastern restaurant or belly dancing class for a referral. Better yet: got a brave friend? Let her (okay, maybe him) brush up on a few moves and lead your guests in some lessons. Barring that, slip a belly-dancing instructional video into the VCR/DVD and see who's brave enough to start things off.

Fast-action card games round out the entertainment. Spit and War are two of my favorites. It's not about an involved card game, just a little side action to get guests interacting. That doesn't mean there is no room for betting. But you may be surprised by what your guests will wager!

flirting.

Belly dancers usually receive tips in a variety of places when they're dancing (cleavage, top edge of harem pants, etc.). When the person you have your eye on is shaking it with the rest of the belly-dancing crowd, slip 'em your telephone number instead of cash.

If you're at a loss for what to say to someone you've got your eye on, take the simple approach. Look at the object of your attention, say hello, look at him/her with a devilish grin, and challenge them to a staring contest. Don't laugh; if they like you, they'll be into it.

soundtrack.

There are of course all kinds of choices in classic Moroccan music to set the mood. It's hard to go wrong, so hit the international section of your record store and let the coolest covers guide you. You could try a belly dancing album, like *The Rough Guide to Bellydance* from World Music Network. There are also more modern Arabic-European crossover sets, like *Arabic Groove* (from Putomayo World Music), *Arabesque* (Gut), or *Arabian Travels* (Six Degrees). You could go for Algerian raï music (a lot of its practitioners, like Cheb Khaled, make Paris their base). Electronic groups like Transglobal Underground have a string of albums—their Egyptian singer Natacha Atlas has several solo albums. But you don't have to play Arab beats all night; vintage flamenco compilations evoke the same feeling because of Spain's Moorish past—and it's the sexiest music going. If you're going straight for the hip, check out the Buddha Bar compilations that feature Arabic-flavored tunes alongside European and African sounds.

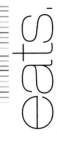

lettuce-wrapped meatballs
serves about 10

for the meatballs

- ½ cup ground pork, beef, chicken, or lamb
- 1 scallion, chopped
- 2 tablespoons sesame seeds
- 2 tablespoons chopped cilantro
- ⅛ teaspoon each of all-spice, clove, coriander, cumin, and ginger

for cooking

- 1¼ teaspoons cornstarch
- 3 tablespoons vegetable oil

to serve

- 20 baby romaine or butter lettuce leaves
- Cilantro for garnish
- Bottled chili sauce, for dipping

Mix all ingredients for the meatballs together and form into 20 balls. Sprinkle the cornstarch on a tray and roll the balls until lightly coated. Heat the oil in a frying pan over medium heat and cook the meatballs until golden brown and cooked through. Remove from heat and let drain on paper towels. Place each ball on a lettuce leaf and garnish with cilantro. Place a bowl with the chili sauce nearby for dipping.

grocery store eats.

Load a ton of pistachios into a big bowl and place a smaller bowl alongside it for discarded shells. Set out an assortment of olives and stuffed dolmas (grape leaves filled with rice) from the deli counter. Offer bowls of hummus and babaganoush (Middle Eastern dips) with pita bread. Skewer cubes of feta cheese and cucumber seasoned with olive oil, fennel seeds, and cracked black pepper. Nougat and dried apricots and dates filled with goat cheese are perfect for a small assortment of sweets.

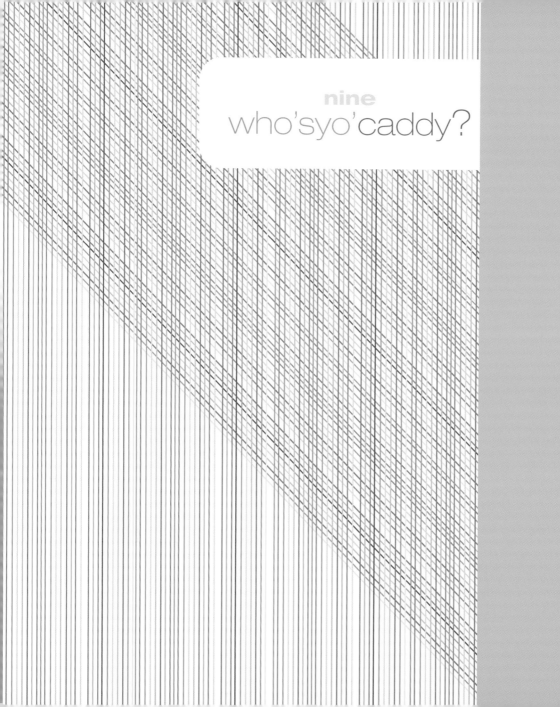

nine
who'syo'caddy?

If I saw myself dressed like that, I'd have to kick my own ass.
—*HAPPY GILMORE*

a beer-and-scotch-tasting invitational at the 19th hole

Golf is a highly addictive game that requires serious concentration and the patience of Buddha. Its stodgy traditions make it ripe for a little shakedown. Golf is the quietest game with the loudest clothing, and it's time to even up that relationship. "Bad plaid and uptight attitudes will not keep us out of the game," says Mitch Marine, musician and avid golfer. "Exclusivity is boring." With this in mind, party people, it's time to go pro. Mix up the Most Likely to enter the *Playboy* Scramble crowd with the Golf Channel crowd, blow up some Bud Light plastic chairs, and watch the spectacle. At this event, PGA stands for "Party Goes All Night," so bone up on the three B's—Beer, Booze, and Betting—and turn your crib into the 19th hole. On this course, the golf is just the excuse.

booze.

tiger

Because of their varying weights, the beers remain separated and the drink ends up looking like a striped—well, tiger.

serves 2

- 1 bottle amber ale or hard cider beer
- 1 bottle stout beer

Fill glass ½ full with ale or cider beer, then top with stout.

beer and scotch tasting.

beer * Introduce the group to a variety of off-the-wall and traditional brews. Here is the breakdown. Ale-styles include Scottish-style heavy ale, German-style Hefeweizen, and Belgian-style fruit lambic. Ales like Arrogant Bastard, Road Dog, Tilted Kilt, HopDevil, Lindemans Pêche, and Samuel Adams Weiss Biere will give tasters something to talk about. Lager-styles include American-style lager, dry lager, and ice (beer) lager. Try favorites like Moosehead Lager, Boehemian Blonde, Asahi Draft, Kirin Ichiban, and Molson Ice. Try New England–style ciders like Woodchuck Granny Smith Draft Cider and Dry Blackthorn Cider. Spice beer is unique and specific in flavor. Check out Rogue Yellow Snow Ale or Post Road Pumpkin Ale to get an idea of what this category is all about.

scotch * A scotch tasting is easy to set up. Grab a variety (three will do) of single malts from different regions of Scotland: Speyside, Islay, Highlands, and Lowlands. A scotch specialist at your local deli or liquor store can help you find the best variety in your price range. Check out the Macallan, Glenlivet, Bowmore, Glenmorangie, and Glenkinchie brands. Pour about an ounce into a small glass, sniff it, add a splash of room-temperature water, sniff it again, and taste it. You're looking (um, tasting) for: esters like fruit and flowers; phenols that are medicinal, peaty, or smoky; aldehydes like hay, grass, and leather; sweetness like vanilla, toffee, and honey; grains like malt and wheat; oils like butter, hazels, and walnuts; woods like cedar and pine.

invites.

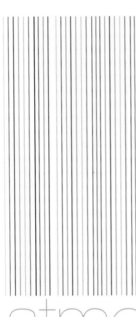

Make up a tweaked-out club membership policy. Send it via e-mail or print it out and snail-mail it:

You are invited to participate in the [insert your name] Inaugural Beer-and-Scotch-Tasting Invitational, to be held at [insert location] on [insert date] at [insert time].

This invitation comes with a complimentary membership in The Golf Punks Association. Adherence to it's rules is required for admittance:

1. Dress Code—No visible animal logos, cardigans, cuffed shorts, or periwinkle-hued anything.

2. Code of Conduct—No equipment narcissists or ball busting allowed (okay, mild ball busting is permitted within the boundaries of bad taste).

3. Privileges—Members are allowed to bring guests to club functions (as long as they're not total stiffs).

Notice: Membership has its privileges. Let the club manager know by [insert RSVP date] how many will be in your group [insert telephone number and/or e-mail address for RSVPs].

atmosphere.

Golf might be the one sport where athletic performance can actually rise along with alcohol consumption. So get your clubhouse in shape thinking Love Shack meets *Caddyshack*. Hang a sign that reads FREE YOUR MIND AND YOUR SWING WILL FOLLOW, wherever your guests will arrive.

Start with the bar. Take a couple of galvanized steel trash cans and lay planks on top of them to create a counter space. Stuff the bottom two-thirds of the trash cans with empty boxes and other clean fill material. Place a sturdy plastic bag over the stuffing and fill it with ice and bottles of beer, soda, and water. Use the area on the planks to hold your tasting gear: a couple of bottle openers, glasses, bottles of scotch, bar towels, nibbles, and napkins. If you're not into the trash can idea, just lay a strip of hideous plaid fabric over a table to make the bar. Somewhere close

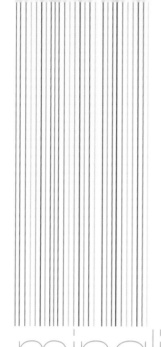

(but not too close) to the bar, place a bucket for bottle cap flicking. You'll be amazed at the wide variety of techniques cap-snapping guys have perfected, and they love showing golf babes their form.

A bit of AstroTurf ups the green factor, so lay a patch wherever you need a little more atmosphere. (It's also perfect for stain camouflage. It can be picked up at home improvement centers and hardware stores.) Burn candles, spray room freshener, or hang car odorizers with a "fresh cut grass" scent.

Crash your local thrift or trophy shops and load up on old loving cups, crystal bowls, award plaques, and ribbons to use as prizes for party games and clubhouse décor. If desired, write a new label to cover old lettering on the pieces with your own version of the award: best use of divot as hairpiece, most likely to get kicked off the course, highest score on the front nine, most creative use of profanity, etc.

mingling

Work on your short game: get your guests interacting by setting up a hole-in-one putting contest. Pick an area of the party where you have room to make it difficult enough to be fun, then set up one hole for partyers to try to make in one shot. Sporting goods stores sell miniature golf sets that are perfect for this kind of thing. The golf bandits in the group are sure to turn it into a Vegas-style wagering opportunity. Just sit back and wait for the trash talk to begin. At country clubs, they often give a brand-new car to the lucky shot. In this case, a Matchbox Jag will do.

Identifying your golf ball from the others flying around a course can make you crazy. Send players home with their own distinctive version by setting up a ball-marking station to customize the little devils. Fill a galvanized bucket with golf balls. Then pile paint pens, multicolored permanent markers, tattoos, stickers, etc. around the bucket and watch as your guests access their inner artist; flames, burning hearts, and Japanese symbols are a few ideas for customization.

soundtrack.

There's something about golf that screams "Eighties!" even though the punks didn't really start hitting the links until the '90s. Maybe it's the plaids and polos, the country club excess, *Caddyshack*'s undeniable status as a classic, or maybe because that's the last time candy-ass pink was fashion currency on the street with both men and women, Republican fund-raisers and New Wave club stars alike.

That said, this party is the perfect excuse to haul out the '80s New Wave compilations. You could stay up watching late-night TV, waiting for the inevitable infomercial to pop up on your screen to find one. In the meantime, here's a little list to help:

Bands: Duran Duran, Blondie, New Order, Devo, Split Enz, Joe Jackson, Madness, the Bangles, Bauhaus, and Depeche Mode for the moodier set. Squeeze, Scritti Politi, the Pet Shop Boys, The Cure, Echo and the Bunnymen, Talking Heads, and Elvis Costello for the rest.

Don't forget: Blondie's "11:59," Lena Lovich's "New Toy," Bow Wow Wow's "I Want Candy," The Romantics' "What I Like About You," Romeo Void's "Never Say Never" which features the unforgettable line, "I'd like you better if we slept together," "Rock Lobster" by the B-52's—and no '80s retro moment is complete without Frank Zappa's "Valley Girl" throbbing in the background.

Best Bet: Rhino Records has you covered with *Millennium: 80's New Wave Party* and *Dance Hits of the 80's* and, for those who can't stop there, the *Like, Omigod! The '80's Pop Culture Box,* a deluxe, seven-disc opus covering the entire decade's pop music.

grocery store eats.

Line galvanized buckets of various sizes with newspaper and load them up with Terra Chips, flavored pretzels, and your specialty divot mix—peanuts, sunflower and pumpkin seeds, etc. Grab some frozen beer-battered or spiced onion rings and prepare them according to the directions on the package. Then load them into newspaper cones (the sports section is perfect). Just roll the paper into a cone and secure the edge with tape or a sticker.

cobb salad sandwiches

makes 16 small sandwiches

3 tablespoons Dijon mustard

3 tablespoons red wine vinegar

⅔ cup olive oil

Salt and pepper, to taste

3 pounds cooked chicken (substitute crab or lobster if you want to go all out)

1 head iceberg lettuce, cut into strips

2 hard-boiled eggs, roughly chopped

2 slices bacon, cooked and diced

2 ounces blue cheese, crumbled

2 tomatoes, chopped

¼ cup roughly chopped parsley

1 avocado, peeled and cubed

1 loaf sliced sandwich bread or 4 large, round sandwich rolls

To make the vinaigrette, mix the mustard and vinegar together. Whisk in the olive oil, season with salt and pepper to taste, and set aside.

For the salad, season the chicken with salt and pepper and toss with 3 tablespoons of the vinaigrette. Set aside. In a bowl, mix together the lettuce, eggs, bacon, blue cheese, tomatoes, parsley, and avocado. Season with salt and pepper and lightly coat with the remaining vinaigrette. Keep the chicken and the salad mixtures separate.

To assemble, toast eight slices of the bread or the sandwich rolls. Pile the salad mixture on first, then the chicken, then a piece of bread on top. Slice into quarters and chow down!

ten

paging doctor
bombay

Doctor, doctor, won't you please prescribe me somethin'
A day in the life of someone else? —PINK

a prescription for pressing flesh and mixing tonic

diagnosis: Early warning signs include a lowered sense of humor and general beigeness. But when symptoms of exhaustion from urban chaos, office politics, minglephobia, or workaholism explode into full-blown burnout, it doesn't necessarily mean a mad dash to the therapist is in order. Take a page in bedside manners from Dr. Feelgood. Priority one on the treatment chart is immediate exposure to other sufferers—and resuscitating the dying art of conversation. In other words, when people chat about what's freaking other people out, it takes their mind off what's freaking *them* out. Sometimes the cure is as simple as filling a prescription to party.

booze,
alternative medicine

serves about 16

1 750-ml bottle gin

4 branches fresh rosemary, washed

1 375-ml bottle sweet vermouth

¼ cup lemon juice

¼ cup simple syrup (see p. 67)

Lemon wheels and fresh rosemary, for garnish

Tonic water for mixing

Place the rosemary branches into the bottle of gin and let infuse for several hours in the refrigerator. Pour the gin (without the rosemary) into a pitcher along with the vermouth, lemon juice, and simple syrup. Stir and leave in the freezer for an hour or so. To serve, garnish the pitcher with lemon wheels and fresh rosemary and set out with a bottle of chilled tonic water on the bar for guests to mix up themselves.

invites,

Notify patients to check in by sending an announcement that mimics a prescription: Use five-inch-square white paper and write that big "Rx" symbol on the top. Don't forget to use terrible handwriting (if necessary, include a translation from the nurse). It could go something like this:

Rx:	A Prescription to Party
Physician:	Dr. Bombay for [your name]
Date to Be Filled:	[Party date]
Medication:	Cocktails and hors d'oeuvres to restore circulation, maybe a few shots, depending on severity of condition.
Dosage:	Starting at 8:00 P.M.: [party time]
Possible Interactions:	Side effects include excitement, a loss of inhibitions, and uncontrollable fits of laughing.
Office:	[Address of party]
Confirmation #:	[RSVP information]

atmosphere,

Instead of transforming your whole house into a doctor's office (although some plastic plants and *Highlights* magazine might augment the vibe), focus your efforts on stocking the "pharmacopoiea." Make the bar self-service so guests can play Mr. Pharmacist, while you oversee the mingling progress and check for vital signs. Checklist:

* Recipe book named "Thirst Aid," filled with your favorite drink recipes along with the ingredients to make them. Here are a few drink names to use when compiling other recipes for your book: Cat Scan, Transfusion, Flu Shots, Wet Nurse, Wonder Drug, Beeper.

* Clear glass or stainless steel ice bucket, tongs, and a few white bar towels (dish towels are perfect).

* Jigger, bottle/wine opener, cocktail shaker, and strainer.

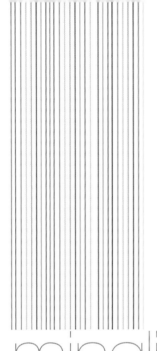

* Pitcher, glasses, and/or test tubes for shots—pick up the test tubes from floral supply companies (they use them for single-stem vases), gourmet food shops (they use them for storing herbs), or a well-stocked barware store.

When expanding your décor horizons, think old-school pharmaceutical: apothecary jars filled with candies (Mentos, Hot Tamales, and white gumballs) that look medicinal. Use anatomy diagrams and eye charts on the wall as a background for a photo op. Fill vases with fresh herbs instead of flowers (unless you want it to look like someone's really sick). Find the apothecary jars at mass merchandisers or bed and bath shops. Anatomy diagrams and eye charts can be found at toy stores or medical supply houses.

For visual ambience, turn the sound off the boob tube and roll episodes on the VCR or DVD of television shows like *ER*, *Emergency*, or *Scrubs*, or movies like *The English Patient* or *M*A*S*H*.

mingling

For some, a social gathering is as scary as a trip to the doctor. Your job is to ease that anxiety. Dig up that vintage board game *Operation* and give a prize for Best Surgeon. A stethoscope can be a fun prop, too (is there a sexier icebreaker than asking to listen to someone's heartbeat?).

Design an ID bracelet–making station, a takeoff on hospital wristbands. Start with thick vellum paper and cut it into strips long enough to fit around a variety of wrists (vellum is see-through paper found at office or art supply stores). Attach a piece of Velcro to each end of the bracelet (one end with the "female" side and one end with the "male") to create the clasp (pick up Velcro tape at fabric stores). Then, with different colors of fine-tip permanent markers, guests can write a quick mantra on their bracelet, along the lines of LOVE IS LIKE OXYGEN, PEACE, RESPECT, AVAILABLE, or their phone numbers.

Hip your patients to the benefits of aromatherapy with an assortment of essential oils, placed on a serving tray garnished with fresh herbs and flowers (like lavender, rosemary, and jasmine). Include a glossary of the healing powers they

are thought to possess: lemongrass heals headaches, marigold helps ulcers, rose is an aphrodisiac, and clary sage helps with stress. Tiny, inexpensive vials can double as party favors.

Get little votives and make smaller versions of those big glass candles with images of saints and prayers that bring luck or wealth or love. With your friends in mind, think of some useful things to write in silver or gold paint markers on the side of the candle. Maybe it's NEW JOB or NO MORE BAD HAIR DAYS or DUMP HIM! It could get flirty when guests start fighting over them. Suggest an arm wrestle.

soundtrack.

There's only one thing that feels good to an achin' heart and that's a song about an achin' heart. And the only place you'll find more broken hearts per square inch than a Hank Williams record is in a stack of vintage soul records. And while Hank waters down his beer with tears, the ladies of soul have a better solution: they will survive, in the words of Gloria Gaynor. So get out the platters filled with lines like "Who do you think you are, Mr. Big Stuff?" (Jean Knight) and "Respect Yourself" (Staple Singers). Rhino Records (www.rhino.com) is your one-stop shopping spot for this (and basically all your other party music needs). Check out *Go Girl! Soul Sisters Tellin' It Like It Is* with songs like "Your Turn to Cry" by Betty LaVette and "You're the Dog" by Irma Thomas. And of course, the queen of soul—Aretha Franklin. Every girl should always have two things: a bottle of Champagne in her refrigerator and an Aretha Franklin record.

lip service serves about 15

Prepare one box of red Jell-O according to package directions, but substitute vodka for half the water. Stir in one box of Knox gelatin for every box of Jell-O, pour the mixture into a sheet pan, and chill until set. Cut out shooters with a cookie cutter (ideally, a lip-shaped one) and serve in paper cups with a great bedside manner.

eats.

non-cardiac crudités with bloody mary tomatoes

serves about 12

2 cups red and yellow cherry tomatoes

1 cup vodka

1¼ tablespoons Worcestershire sauce

13 dashes Tabasco sauce

1 clove crushed garlic

Salt and pepper to taste

1 teaspoon fresh rosemary, chopped

12 asparagus spears, blanched

12 baby carrots, peeled with the stem left on, then blanched

1 small bunch wax beans, blanched (about 5 ounces)

3 small cucumbers, peeled and cut lengthwise into quarters

1 pound edamame, fresh or frozen (blanched according to package directions)

For the Bloody Mary Tomatoes: Cut a small cross on the bottom of each tomato and place in a bowl. Add the vodka, Worcestershire, Tabasco, and garlic to the tomatoes. Mix gently, cover, and leave in the refrigerator overnight. Drain the tomatoes and sprinkle with salt, pepper, and rosemary.

For the crudités: Arrange an assortment of the prepared vegetables on a platter. Place the Bloody Mary Tomatoes in a small bowl in the center of the platter. Serve with a variety of your favorite bottled salad dressings decanted into small bowls surrounding the vegetable platter.

grocery store eats.

Assemble sliced smoked salmon on toasted brioche smeared with cream cheese that has been flavored with fresh dill and lemon juice.

95

acknowledgments

It takes a posse to create a book, and I'd like to thank the crew who dug in and helped me out:

Tanya Mallean and Bill Skrzniarz, the smooth, brainiac attorneys who always have my back. • Lauren Oliver, an artist and smarty-pants who has influenced me in such a good way. Thank you for your intelligent words and killer music. • Vanessa Torres (she's just Nessy from the block), a gifted writer who jumped right in when the deadlines got tight. • Mitchell Kamark, who hooked me up with the right crowd. • Kim McCabe, who started it all for me. • Julia Cameron who doesn't know that she helped me write this book with the simple words "writing is about getting something down, not making something up." Kevin Dornin and Tina Rupp, the image-makers who photographed this book and gave much more than I ever expected. • "Miss Food Stylist" Megan Fawn Schlow and prop stylist Stephanie Basralian, who not only made the shots but who are generous with their talents and themselves. • Gary Hill, a designer, stylist, and friend who is so talented that I always hope a little bit rubs off on me. • Robin Gerts and Tom Blumenthal of Geary's Beverly Hills for the use of their exquisite crystal, china, and silver. • Alec Lestr, Joachim Splichal, and Alain Vergnault of Patina Group for their generosity and creative culinary expertise. • Steve Wallace and Mike Escobar of Wally's Liquors for their smooth bartending and drink tips. • Pottery Barn, Front Gate, and Regal Rents for the use of their products featured in this book.

Special thanks to the players in the Clarkson Potter house: Pam Krauss, the bigwig editor who gave me the chance. • Adina Steiman, the sweet editor who took all the flack and kept the peace. • Art director Marysarah Quinn and Jan Derevjanik, the designer who masterminded the famous *Flirtini* stripe. • Leigh Ann Ambrosi, the public relations guru and friend from way back who steered me to Clarkson Potter, and Kate Harris, the publicist who believed enough for all of us. • Amy Boorstein, managing editor, Linnea Knollmueller, production manager, and Susan Westendorf, production editor, who don't miss a trick.

Thanks to my circle of friends who inspired this book:

Lin Milano (whose lips appear on the cover), my manager, confidant, voice of reason, sexy role model, recipe tester, and most of all my friend who reminds me not to worry about being hip or cool, worry about being human. • Tom Milano, my buddy who surfs QVC with me, cracks me up, and shows me that sometimes it doesn't need to be more complicated than a good, cold beer (however, there's no reason it can't be a low carb experience). • Lysse Girl, the pepper in our salt and pepper routine who embraces my geeky side, taught me how to wear cleavage, and who floors me with her big heart on a regular basis. • CoCo, a brilliant music supervisor who thinks he's an anti-partier, but really he's the one that everyone in the room wants to talk to, myself included. • Uncle Mitch, a walking party who has a margarita machine, sombrero, and Elvis music with him at all times. • Alec Ledd, Star of Stage and Screen. A jet-set socialite who promises to teach me how to talk my way into any club, anywhere, period. • Linda and Roland Fasel, my friends who are responsible for starting my career in books and for making me a godmother. • Aunt Allana—The Big A, who always told me I better get our name in print. • Ringworm Renee, my sweet friend who took me to my first parties—I guess they had more of an impact then I thought! • Mom, thank you for your unconditional adoration. It's never a bad thing for a writer, or a daughter. • Luigi Bellometti, who taught me how to entertain, make risotto and the only person I've ever seen drink red wine and cola... together. • Jim Baroni. My husband who gets so nervous throwing parties that I wrote this book for him. I love you forever.